Newcastle-under-Lyme

in old picture postcards

by
Paul J. Bemrose

European Library - Zaltbommel/Netherlands MCMLXXXIII

Acknowledgements:
The author wishes to thank the following private collectors and institutions for permission to reproduce these prints:
Author: 83.
Borough Museum: 1, 2, 3, 9, 13, 16, 19, 26, 28, 29, 30, 34, 35, 42, 45, 46, 50, 53, 56, 58, 59, 63, 64, 65, 66, 68, 71, 73, 75, 76, 78, 79, 80, 85, 91, 92, 95, 96, 97, 99, 100, 103, 105, 107, 108, 112, 113, 114, 115, 116, 117, 118, 120, 121, 122, 123, 124.
Bourne J. Esq.: 70.
Butler F. Esq.: 4, 5, 6, 14, 15, 20, 22, 23, 32, 38, 39, 40, 41, 60, 62, 84, 88, 89, 109, 111.
Chadwick S.T. Esq.: 119.
Morris D. Esq.: 8, 11, 21, 25, 33, 37, 47, 48, 52, 67, 87, 106, 110.
Newcastle Library: 17, 24, 27, 31, 36, 43, 44, 51, 54, 55, 57, 61, 69, 77, 81, 82, 86, 90, 93, 98, 101, 102, 104.
Rogers F. Esq.: 7, 10, 12, 18, 49, 72, 74.
Warrilow E. Esq.: 94.

List of Principal Publishers of Newcastle picture postcards:
Local: Bagguley, G.T.; Blakeman C.D.; Briggs & Co.; Deakin C.H.; Edwards; Harrison E.; Mandley & Unett and Parton W.
National: Boots (Cash Carry Chemists); 'Collectorcard'; Doncaster Rotophoto Ltd.; Friths; 'Hartmann' Series; Jackson & Sons Grimsby; Lilywhite; Shaw W.; Templeman; Trent Bridge Publishing Co.; Tuck Raphael Ltd.; Valentines; Woolf Stewart Co. and 'Wrench' Series.

GB   ISBN 90 288 2455 3

European Library in Zaltbommel/Netherlands publishes among other things the following series:

IN OLD PICTURE POSTCARDS *is a series of books which sets out to show what a particular place looked like and what life was like in Victorian and Edwardian times. A book about virtually every town in the United Kingdom is to be published in this series. By the end of this year about 75 different volumes will have appeared. 1,250 books have already been published devoted to the Netherlands with the title* **In oude ansichten.** *In Germany, Austria and Switzerland 500, 60 and 15 books have been published as* **In alten Ansichten;** *in France by the name* **En cartes postales anciennes** *and in Belgium as* **En cartes postales anciennes** *and/or* **In oude prentkaarten** *150 respectively 400 volumes have been published.*

For further particulars about published or forthcoming books, apply to your bookseller or direct to the publisher.

This edition has been printed and bound by Grafisch Bedrijf De Steigerpoort in Zaltbommel/Netherlands.

INTRODUCTION

It is perhaps fortunate for this publication that the borough has within the past decade celebrated the 800th anniversary of its foundation in 1173. The celebrations were organised in 1973 and designed to make its citizens aware of the rich heritage that is every Newcastilian's birthright. As a consequence, there has been a steady increase in interest in learning more about the social and industrial growth of Newcastle and its community, particularly insofar as the later period of Victorian England is concerned and also those years leading up to the outbreak of World War I. These eras marked a time when the town was showing early signs of changing its physical appearance after many years of relative stagnation. By 1880, the development of photography had advanced technologically almost beyond recognition from the early faltering attempts of Daguerre in the late 1830's and Fox Talbot's equally rather limited calotype system whereby he was able to produce paper negatives and prints. As the decade advanced, photography had become almost a way of life in Victorian England, not least in Newcastle, so that by the time 1880 had arrived and George Eastman marketed his first 'Kodak' camera, the era of the 'snapshot' had been ushered in, giving rise to many aspiring and often gifted amateur photographers. Informal and candid camera studies using this and similar systems which no longer required long time exposures, revealed for the first time the true quality of contemporary life in towns, cities and the countryside.

Sir Benjamin Stone was one such gifted recorder of the contemporary scene in Great Britain and he produced over thirty thousand plates for posterity to wonder at and admire. On the local scene, such professional photographers as A.W. Harrison who was also one of the first to take photographs in 1896 using the new Röntgen rays or X-rays as they are better known to aid in medical diagnosis and surgery, W. Parton, another well established photographer, and the firm of G.T. Bagguley were all printing local views. Several national companies also produced local cards.

The majority of the illustrations contained herein have been carefully selected to emphasise this new and important development which allowed the camera the ability to capture the event as it really was and not posed as was often the case previously.

Picture postcards were produced primarily by photographic studios and printing firms to make money and they rapidly became a lucrative side line in the general stock-in-trade of such establishments. As pictorial souvenirs, subject matter was naturally enough generally though not always made to look as attractive as possible to the purchaser. Not infrequently, photos were either retouched or vignetted to mask out unwanted or ugly detail. Many old Newcastle views have been treated in this manner. Despite this, a few such examples have been included either because they are rare prints in their own right, or because they depict an unusual shot not reproduced elsewhere.

Because a prolifically illustrated history of the town was produced by the council in 1973, care has been taken in this publication to duplicate as few photos as possible found therein. This has inevitably resulted in variations in print quality since the author has had to look much further afield for illustrations and use prints which in some cases are photo copies or even copies of photo copies. It is hoped the reader will forgive some of the quality in the interest of pictorial variety.

Because this book contains a large number of hitherto unpublished photographs, it virtually becomes an essential adjunct to the Borough Council's 1973 'Octocentenary' history book. It will provide many hours of visual information and pleasure to the serious student of local history and casual reader alike.

Newcastle never has enjoyed a reputation as a tourist attraction and for this reason the range of picture postcards produced throughout the period under review, has proved to be somewhat limited. Similarly, industrial views are comparatively uncommon.

Within recent years, television has played a not insignificant part in making the public increasingly aware of the satisfaction and pleasure that can be acquired through learning about industrial archaeology and social history. A great deal of research has been produced recently by the professional and amateur historian alike. Fortunately, by dint of a more enlightened approach to the subject, much of what is left to us of our industrial heritage is now not so frequently subjected to what used often to be a sudden and inevitable total annihilation by the bulldozer.

Newcastle lies on the western flank of the North Staffordshire Coal Field. It enjoys along with its neighbours the dubious appellation, an 'industrial town of the North Midlands'. The heavy extractive industries of coal and iron, plus brick and tile making formed the mainstay of its early eighteenth and nineteenth century industrial development. Felt hat making, brewing, silk and cotton processing were also much in evidence. Oddly enough, the borough never became a 'pottery town' in the strict meaning of the phrase although much of its workforce was being absorbed into the pottery industry by the 1880's: it did however have one or two potters of note operating at various periods in the borough.

The bulk of the towns basic trades and industries were particularly productive in the decades leading up to the turn of the present century. Trade and commerce originally developed because of Newcastle's strategic position astride the main thoroughfare from London to Carlisle. This route had become well established by the thirteenth century and it rapidly evolved into an important market town and has maintained this position for the past six centuries. What has been stated may suggest that the Newcastle of the late nineteenth and early twentieth centuries presented a dismal 'Lowrie' type industrial landscape with nothing to relieve the unmitigated gloom. Happily this was not the case as hopefully many of the photographs will shew.

Even when all its heavy peripheral industrial production was at a peak, the beautiful and not infrequently sylvan Staffordshire countryside was never very far away for those who sought it. The population of the town which in 1880 was 17,500 increased by only some six thousand during the fifty years covered by this book. After 1930 however, large boundary changes were soon to take place and the town grew in importance economically and politically almost out of recognition. Today, the borough supports a population in excess of one hundred and twenty thousand souls.

Town directories and guide books are always a useful source of information and from them we can trace what improvements have been taking place over a period of years. For example, in 1881 the silk, cotton and paper mills were all operating, the sugar refinery was expanding and working at full capacity. The town had three breweries, three corn mills and two saw mills in production. The Enderley mill, founded by Richard Stanway in 1881 was operating as a model textile mill and included a surgery, creche, reading room and savings bank.

By 1900 the new Municipal Hall had been in operation for over a decade, the town had a free library, school of art and a fine public swimming bath was built in 1906. Gas supplies (1880) and electricity (1904) were being produced by the Council's own plant although it should be mentioned that the town was one of the first to be provided privately with gas in 1819.

At the close of the period, we find that Newcastle was commencing an expansion in a westerly direction to satisfy the demand for high class residential dwellings from industrialists from the pottery towns and the surrounding area. Its popularity long established as a 'dormitory' town was growing. Light industrial development was taking root and the traditional markets and shopping facilities were as much in demand as ever.

1. The borough's principal street lines had become firmly established by the first couple of decades of the nineteenth century. Most of the landmarks which are depicted on artistic representations such as this by J. Hulse painted in 1800 and published in 1900 and later photographic studies, were well in evidence by 1825. Many of the ensuing plates will show that despite quite radical changes to several ground and first floor frontages, basic structures can frequently be identified, modified though they have been to suit changing times and architectural styles.

2. The restored mediaeval market cross about 1880. Focal point of mayor choosing ceremonies, 'Mock Mayor' making events and civic proclamations throughout the nineteenth century. The cross appears to have been originally sited in the High Street facing the top of the Ironmarket but it had been repositioned at the north end of the Guildhall by 1820 in which year it also received its decorative wrought iron lighting fixture.

3. Market day in the High Street 1880. Traditional site of the town's markets and fairs. Well depicted are 'the stones' or street cobbles now long since gone but still referred to by many when they speak of the street market. By 1882, a steam tramcar system was operating in Newcastle, later to be succeeded by an electric tram service. The original borough police station, the Old Roebuck posting inn and the Castle Hotel, which by 1834 had also become a post house, can all be clearly seen in this view.

High Street, Newcastle-under-Lyme

4. The Guildhall has for well over two centuries dominated the High Street from all directions. It was here until recently that the town council held its meetings. Quarter Sessions Courts were also convened here. Happily custom has not been completely lost because the town burgesses still continue to meet in this their traditional home. Erected in 1714 it replaces an earlier town hall of Tudor origin which had been sited in a more northerly direction, adjacent to the top of the Ironmarket. Originally the Guildhall was open on the ground floor and was used to provide space for a provision market until 1854 when the new covered market was built to improve this facility.

Town Hall and Market Place. Newcastle.

5. New forms of street furniture appeared in town with the introduction of an electric tram service in the early 1900's. Such innovations gave the highways a completely new look with its permanent ways and cable supporting columns. In some measure this new system tended to bring orderliness to the regulation of vehicles and carriages using the town centre since such traffic was now obliged to keep large areas occupied by the tramways clear at all times. Cable strain plates and the old P.E.T. Company post marking plates can still be found by diligently searching for them on old walls and buildings.

NEWCASTLE STAFFS

6. Now demolished, the three storied block to the right of the old Manchester & Liverpool Bank was for many years occupied by the council's town clerk's department until it removed to Derwent House in The Brampton before being finally integrated in the civic offices in Merrial Street. This photograph was taken about 1912 and shows that part of Penkhull Street (since 1954 incorporated into the High Street) almost opposite the Golden Lion public house.

7. Produced in 1927, the following sequence of three cards was published by the Doncaster Rotophoto Co. Ltd. Only the lamp on the Market Cross appears to have been altered since it was re-sited by the Guildhall in the 1820's. The 'Kings Theatre' to the right of the Guildhall seems to be screening a silent Charlie Chaplin film. This theatre was soon destined to change its name to the 'Savoy' cinema complete with its own self-contained twelve table billiards saloon to vie for patrons with the then novel two screen picture house a little higher up the road in Red Lion Square known as the 'Regal and Pavilion' and owned by Bob Beresford, an Alderman and ex-mayor of the town.

8. Evidence of increasing vehicular traffic on the roads can be seen from this card where cars and lorries, even a primitive petrol tanker are parked in front of the Castle Hotel. Horse drawn carts and carriages as well as the electric tramway were soon doomed to redundancy by the rapid increase in bus undertakings and private cars, in fact, the tram system was abandoned in 1928.

PENKHULL ST. NEWCASTLE. 127-9

9. A similar view to the previous one but taken from the south end of the former Penkhull Street. The old covered market can be seen on the left by the figures as can the long established but now defunct family hardware business of George Hollins & Sons, (centre right).

High Street, Newcastle.

10. This block of buildings, originally the Roebuck Inn, in the High Street, photographed about 1930 was demolished just prior to World War II. It was replaced by the existing Lancaster Building. Formerly built as a coaching hostelry, it was later converted to accommodate the town's first police station whilst other ground floor areas became shops. The old borough surveyor's office occupied the first floor and one corner of the south end of the building was used as a booking and information office by the up and coming bus undertakings of the Crosville, Midland Red and Potteries companies respectively. The police station was removed to its new premises in Merrial Street in 1936.

HIGH STREET, NEWCASTLE.

11. Two years have elapsed since the paraphernalia of the tram system has been cleared away. This highly evocative study of the north end of the High Street depicts many businesses now long since gone. Kemp's the jewellers, Mandley & Unett, Oxens the chemists and Massey the gunsmith and hardware merchant. A little higher up is the old Boots cash carry chemists where many of the postcards illustrating this book were purchased. Three of the principal cinemas operating in town can also be seen. Only the former Newcastle Cinema later to be known as the 'Plaza' in Nelson Place is missing.

Iron Market &. New Town Hall   Newcastle

12. Perhaps of all the buildings in the Ironmarket the one which caused more outrage and controversy when it was demolished was the Municipal Hall. Opened in 1890 it was designed to replace the Guildhall as a council chamber and also provide accommodation for public functions, a free library and school of art. As the Guildhall dominated the High Street, so the 'Muni' took pride of place with its imposing clocktower in the Ironmarket. Taken in 1910 whilst at the height of its popularity this view is looking toward Nelson Place with King Street beyond.

13. Built as a golden jubilee memorial to Queen Victoria, the Municipal Hall was designed in the 'Flemish' style by a team of North Staffordshire architects. This delightfully informal photo shows the architects and builders making an inspection of the site in 1889.

Queen's Gardens, Newcastle

14. In 1910 the Queen's Gardens were originally enclosed with a high hedge and iron railings. Because of their popularity the gardens were re-designed on a less formal basis and consequently became even more popular between the wars. Well designed flowers beds, borders and intricate carpet bedding became a feature of this pleasance.

...AL HALL, NEWCASTLE-UNDER-LYME

15. By contrast with the previous view, this picture of the gardens taken in 1930 shows that they had been provided with considerably more seats. A band stand had also been built to accommodate regular summer concerts which gradually replaced those formerly given in the Stubbs Walks.

16. Rectory Chambers, Ironmarket 1906. Though still in situ, the fascia has been so radically altered that it is difficult to believe that this building dates back to 1698.

17. A very rare and unusual winter evening portrayal of the Queen's Gardens and Municipal Hall taken from the front of the old borough treasurer's office in 1910.

Ironmarket, Newcastle-Under-Lyme.

18. With the exception of the old Municipal Hall site, almost the first, second and third floor frontages depicted here have remained unaltered however much the street level windows have moved with the times. The site of many old shops can still often be readily identified.

19. Built originally as a late eighteenth century town house, this building stood at the Barracks Road junction with Nelson Place. It was still privately owned in the 1890's but was then acquired by the council for use by its treasurer's department. In the tympanum of its central pediment can be seen a plinth upon which is a bust of Lord Nelson. It seems likely that Nelson Place was named after the bust.

Queen Victoria Statue, Nelson Place, Newcastle-under-Lyme.

20. At one time it was almost impossible to escape a confrontation with the somewhat daunting statue of Queen Victoria when in town. Happily in more recent times she has been relegated from Nelson Place to a quieter part of the suburb. Perhaps more importantly can be seen the original frontage of the Newcastle Theatre before it was converted to the 'Electric Theatre' in 1910.

NELSON SQUARE, NEWCASTLE, STAFFORDSHIRE.

Copyright Lilywhite,
Sowerby Bridge.

21. As the theatre looked in the early thirties, refurbished as the 'Plaza' cinema where the films seemed always to be breaking down. (Note card incorrectly captioned.)

22. It is difficult to imagine the town without its swimming baths, but in fact they are of comparatively recent origin. This card shows the site in Nelson Place. The first town baths were built in School Street in 1852 but soon closed due to mal-administration. The Edward VII Memorial Baths were opened in 1906.

A BIRDS EYE VIEW OF NEWCASTLE.

23. An unusual 'birds eye' view of the Nelson Place area. Probably taken from the tower of the Municipal Hall, it clearly shows that it forms the low lying area at the junction of several roads. Until it was drained at the end of the eighteenth century it was in fact a large tract of reed-girt pool. The theatre was one of the first buildings to be erected after draining what was known as 'Coleshull Lake'.

24. The extent to which the pool occupied the area can be gained from this angle. Taken in front of the Newcastle Theatre about 1904, the rather grand impression it gives of open spaces and leisurely promenades is sadly no longer a feature of this spot.

BRUNSWICK ST NEWCASTLE. 327-29

25. Brunswick Street about 1926 looking towards George Street with the swimming baths on the right. The Palladian styled building on the left became the town's first telephone exchange and also once served as a YMCA hostel.

26. Photographs of Lower Street, one of the older and poorer parts of the town are extremely rare. This 1928 view gives a reasonable impression of what it looked like between the wars. A few industries such as brewing, woodworking and of course the Holborn Paper Mill were operating but basically this was an area of run-down Georgian and Victorian buildings many of which had become 'doss houses'.

27. There were however one or two non-conformist establishments to lend some tone to Lower Street as this snapshot of the Wesleyan Lower Street Chapel illustrates. After 1861, it was taken over by the Methodist Reform Church, a few of whose congregation can be seen in the following plate.

28. A Sunday outing to the country in 1905. This is an interesting study in that it illustrates the apparently wide differences in social strata evident in the party and suggests that the appeal of evangelism at this time was classless.

29. Part of Hinds Vaults, Lad Lane facing the High Street about 1880. Now demolished, this was one of the town's older timber framed buildings. It had a double gabled front, later to be faced with brick and given two projecting windows surmounted by an early cast-iron balustrade.

30. The former junction of Merrial Street with Red Lion Square about 1885. Even a casual glance through the town directories of this period confirms just how well appointed Newcastle was with ale-houses, pubs and off-licences. Mary Ann Williams was a well known licensee and her establishment later to be re-named the 'Happy Land Vaults' was very well patronised indeed as the police report books verify. Next door can be seen 'Pearsons', tailor and hatter, reflecting the towns close association with the production of felt hats which had continued to be the town's staple trade throughout much of the nineteenth century.

31. Church Street from Red Lion Square 1905. Wain's the chemist is another example of a long established family concern reaching into the twentieth century. Note the advertisement in the window for Kodak 'P.O.P' or printing out papers, used by almost every budding amateur photographer in those days.

The Brampton.

Newcastle

Market Place

Ironmarket

The Walks.

32. The 'P.E.T.' tram company used single decker stock exclusively because of the many low bridges to be negotiated in the area. Similarly, there were few double tracks along the system because of road width restrictions, 1907.

33. An interesting group of buildings in the High Street, demolished in the late 1950's, now replaced by Messrs. Woolworth's new store and the covered shopping arcade. The three gabled structure was of a timber framed construction and appears to have had Tudor origins. Taken about 1896, this card well illustrates the miscellany of shops along its frontage and the fact that it was once the Market Inn. To the extreme right of the picture can be seen the opening into Friar Street which in those days was barely wide enough to take a horse and cart.

34. The same area some thirty years later but looking in a southerly direction. The old Market Hall completed in 1854 on the site of the Crown Inn can be seen to the left of the old Woolworth's 'Threepenny and Sixpenny Store'. Part of the rear premises were used in the late nineteenth century as a riding school for 'young gentlefolk'. Later in 1930 it had been converted into a roller skating rink for less gentle pursuits.

35. At the junction of Bridge Street with Liverpool Road there was for many years a working men's clothiers shop known as the 'Northern Stores Clothing Company'. The firm managed to survive into the 1980's but has now closed its doors to customers for ever. Photograph taken about 1910.

36. Being one of the principal market towns in the area, Newcastle could boast many excellent grocers shops not least of whom was H. Watson's provision warehouse in the Ironmarket. In 1907 this is what the shop and its staff looked like. The premises were later taken over by H. Samuel the chain store jewellers. Today, the site is still occupied by this firm.

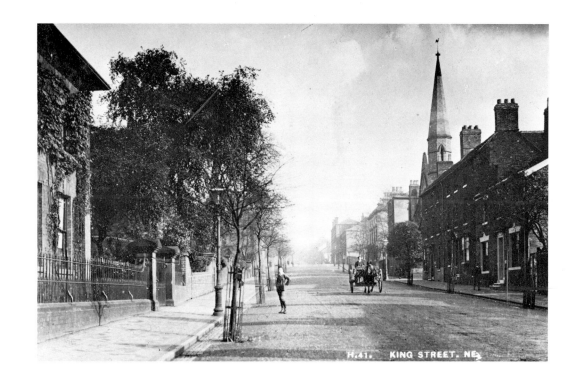

H.41. KING STREET. NE

37. Fortunately for posterity several photographers did not confine their activities to town centre views alone, and as a result many unusual but nevertheless fascinating records of the town's peripheral areas were produced such as this view of King Street taken in 1900 from outside the former town fire brigade headquarters. It shows the vista looking up past the Borough Hotel whose buildings were once part of the Water Street brewery and prior to that, Bulkeley and Bent's potworks.

London Road, Newcastle.

38. Obviously an unposed and heavily re-touched pan of the northern end of London Road about 1900. It shows the terraced houses on the left opposite the Holy Trinity Church which were built on the site of the town's former sugar refinery.

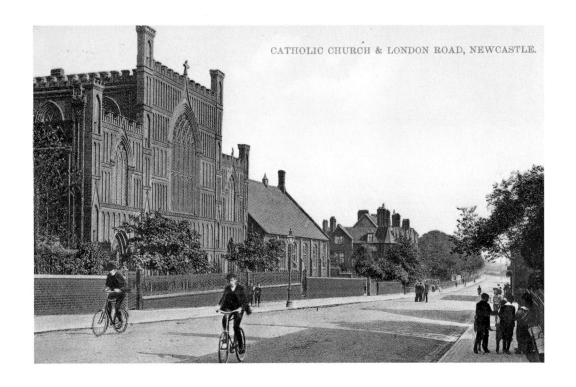

CATHOLIC CHURCH & LONDON ROAD, NEWCASTLE.

39. Post-marked 'August 8th 1910' this view is the reverse of the previous card and shows the southerly aspect of London Road. Traffic problems must have been minimal, since there seem to be no rules of the road being observed by the young cyclists!

London Road, Newcastle

40. London Road about 1929 on the approach to the Old Union Hospital better known today as the 'City General'. The now disused and filled in Lower Canal ran on the other side of the wall to the extreme right of the view.

STUBBS WALKS, NEWCASTLE.

41. An unusual corner of Stubbs Walks in 1908. It hardly does justice to the gardens at all because this is a view of one of the exits! Interestingly though, it does show the site the bed the Upper Canal took from Marsh Parade (in the distance) to its terminus and basin at the opposite end of the Walks.

42. Stubbs Walks with Saint Paul's Church in the distance, taken about 1930. This snapshot has captured the Crimean cannon and World War I tank which kept each other company until 1940 when the latter was removed for scrap as part of the war effort.

43. Vessey Terrace off London Road towards Stubbs Walks.

44. Stubbs Gate with London Road in the middle distance. This photograph was taken in 1910.

45. A dreary part of early nineteenth century Newcastle, euphemistically known as the 'Cherry Orchard' which survived along with other unhealthy parts of the borough for far too long. Situated close to the Ebenezer Chapel, it consisted of rows of cramped workers cottages. Happily the area has now been turned into a car park. The picture dates from about 1928.

THISTLEBERRY HOUSE, NEWCASTLE

46. Thistleberry House, one time home of the Mayer family where Joseph Mayer, the antiquarian collector and philanthropist, was born. The house has recently been replaced by the 'Thistleberry' public house at the Higherland on Keele Road (1896).

47. Descending into Queen Street from the Brampton which remains a highly prized
dormitory area consisting of fine Georgian and Victorian town houses and Villas, Queen
Street leads into Nelson Place. 6-8 Queen Street, now known as 'Mayer House', was owned
by the Mayer family previously mentioned and Thomas Mayer Senior and his son worked
finelessly to secure the granting of the charter of the Royal College of Veterinary
Surgeons in 1844. The veterinary surgery below 6-8 Queen Street on the left of the
photograph was probably the first to be set up in Great Britain.

48. This is another extremely rare card of the late 1920's. It is difficult to imagine why the Higherland was selected as a subject since the area has little of merit to offer nor has it any saving graces whatsoever — except perhaps its people.

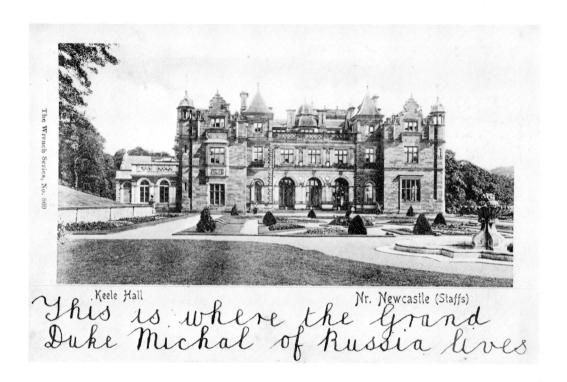

Keele Hall   Nr. Newcastle (Staffs)

This is where the Grand Duke Michal of Russia lives

49. The powerful Sneyd family formerly owned Keele Hall and played a not insignificant part in moulding the history of the town and its surrounding areas. As this card confirms, they acted as host to Grand Duke Michael of Russia whilst on an indefinite stay in England. It was in fact he who was prevailed upon to unveil the statue of Queen Victoria in 1903.

50. Grand Duke Michael himself posing on the Keele Hall steps about 1905.

51. Royal visits always provide occasions where crowds and their reactions can be studied in detail, sometimes with amusing results. Perhaps the most grand and lavish event organised by the town was on the occasion of the visit of King George V and Queen Mary in April 1913, the year before the outbreak of World War I. This is a composite commemorative souvenir of their visit published by W. Shaw of Burslem.

ROYAL VISIT APRIL 1913.
NEWCASTLE. U. LYME.

PHOTO. TEMPLEMAN H

52. Here, an official photograph of the welcoming ceremony.

53. Queen Victoria suitably decorated for the occasion although she still does not look 'amused'.

Royal Visit to Newcastle. 22.4.1913. Decorations in Ironm... 9. Pub. by W.Shaw. Burslem.

54. 'Flying the Flag.'

Royal Visit to Newcastle 22.4.1913. Decorations in Nelson Square 11

55. The whole town was bedecked in bunting and flags. Even a patriotic silent movie had been found and was being screened at the Newcastle cinema to fit the occasion.

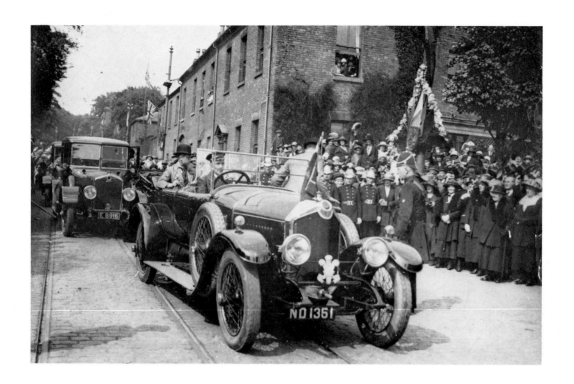

56. Edward, Duke of Windsor and Prince of Wales, was the last royal personality to visit Newcastle before 1930. It was in 1925 that he arrived. Here the royal entourage is entering Nelson Place and about to mount the rostrum just around the corner.

57. An incredulous Prince of Wales looks on as the welcoming speech is delivered. Everyone seems to be slightly amused by what is being said, even the Prince's aide looks unbelieving!

58. Churches have always played a major role in the life of the community. The Parish Church of St. Giles is no exception. This plate illustrates what the former Georgian styled church interior looked like before the new building replaced it in 1876.

59. Simple but pleasing to the eye, the old church was well proportioned and had a splendid gallery. Unfortunately the fabric of the building gave cause for concern in 1872 and Sir Gilbert Scott, an arch Gothic revivalist, was invited to design a new church. Unhappily his plan was accepted and the present sombre and depressing looking edifice was built.

St. George's Church, *Newcastle Staffs.*

Mandley & Unett, *Newcastle Staffs.*

60. Built in 1828 it became a parish church in 1856. The town suffered one or two serious outbreaks of enteric fever in 1847 and two devastating epidemics of cholera in 1832 and 1849. The heavy loss of life caused great concern and steps were taken to improve the town's sanitation. As a result of the loss of life from cholera many of those who died from the disease were buried in this church yard.

61. Looking towards St. George's from Sidmouth Avenue.

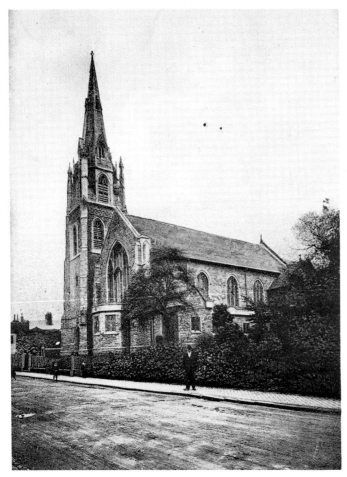

62. Erected basically to serve the needs of a new parish formed in part from St. George's and part Penkhull parish. St. Paul's was built in 1905 and consecrated in 1908.

63. Demolishing the Holborn Paper Mill, August 1890. The site has been associated with the manufacture of paper since about 1811. For much of its life, the mill was owned by the Lamb family who continued in ownership until 1928. A lucrative line for the firm was the production of transfer paper for the pottery industry and the company built up a considerable business in this field.

64. The silk and cotton mills provided employment for hundreds of the town's workforce in the eighteen hundreds. Unfortunately by the end of the century the situation had changed radically and most of the once flourishing mills had either closed or been converted to other uses. The Manchester based United Velvet Cutters Association did however adapt some of the buildings to employ girls in the trade of fustian cutting. The Association continued in business in Newcastle until the late twenties by which time automatic velvet cutting machines had made hand cutting slow and rendered it obsolete. Hempstalls Lane Fustian Mill just prior to World War I.

KNUTTON

65. Brain child of Sir Francis Stanier, mayor and ironmaster in 1851, Knutton Forge was built to extend the output of his industrial empire. The forge was no small venture consisting as it did of sixty puddling furnaces and five rolling mills. The climax of Staniers Empire building was reached in 1864 when he assumed control of the Apedale works, thus making himself undisputed ironmaster and head of the largest iron company in North Staffordshire. By 1930, the year Knutton Forge closed, none of his works remained to bear testimony to his great business acumen.

66. A group of Knutton Forge workers outside one of the rolling mills about 1896.

67. What is probably the only photograph of Knutton Forge showing the works and workers cottages 1906.

68. Despite a recession in the textile and silk processing trades during the closing decades of the last century, Richard Stanway was able to stimulate enough business to found the Enderley Mills in 1881. Designed primarily for making up materials into clothing, it passed into the hands of John Hammond in 1884 who concentrated on the production of military and service uniforms. This firm played a small but crucial role during the First World War by producing enormous quantities of uniforms for the armed services. We see one of the cutting shops about 1915.

69. In common with most other parts of the industrialised Midlands and the North during the General Strike of 1926, this area suffered hardship and depravation on a large scale. Fortunately at least fuel to keep warm was literally available 'for the picking' at many pit-head tips. This became a crucial pass-time for many unemployed families during the period. This picture shows family groups of coal pickers at Apedale, 1926.

70. The demand for town gas was increasing as a result of domestic and industrial demand. The privately owned Brook Street plant was bought out by the borough council in 1880. Surprisingly, the corporation was soon able to extend gas supplies and even sell gas at a reduced rate. Newcastle was one of the first towns in the country to possess street lighting. The first gas undertaking was built at Rye Croft but in 1855 the Brook Street gas works was erected and continued in operation until its demise after World War II. We see gas purifiers being installed about 1930.

NEWCASTLE STATION.

71. Public transport was of course not confined to the roadways. In September 1852 the North Staffordshire Railway Company opened Newcastle Station in King Street. The station entrance was immediately opposite the present Borough Arms Hotel frontage. The line had been brought from Stoke to join up with the older Silverdale and Newcastle Railway at Knutton Junction. Now a leisure walkway with nothing to indicate that the area was once a bustling railway station, this is how the station and its track appeared in 1900.

The Wrench Series, No. 1255

Newcastle
(Staffs).

April 18th 04.

This is not a very good view of our town, but perhaps you will like it. We shall be having more P.C.'s later on

High Street. with love from Gladys M. Slater.

72. The sentiments of the writer may be correct, but at least the card clearly shows the layout of the tramway in the High Street. The view further illustrates a tidier street market layout and another good shot of the 'Stones'.

73. A finely detailed study of one of the company's trams. Newcastle became the centre of routes in the western section through which a large proportion of the 'P.E.T.'s one hundred vehicles operated.

High Street, Newcastle Staffs. Aug: 8th 1904.

Mandley & Unett, Newcastle Staffs.

74. Track in the main consisted of single line stretches with passing loops. The High Street was in fact the systems southerly tram terminus and at the junction of Well Street with Penkhull Street (now the Grosvenor Roundabout) there was a reversing loop. The Newcastle service connected with Chesterton, Silverdale, Hanley, Stoke, Wolstanton, Longport and Burslem.

75. Once the tramways had become obsolescent in the late twenties, it soon became clear that a bus station would have to be provided for the convenience of the omnibus and charabanc user. So many were the private companies and so diverse their routes, that a joint bus terminus came into being not before time in 1932. The 'Beeches', Liverpool Road, before conversion to the town's first bus station about 1924.

76. Early morning at Newcastle Station 1902. A member of the 'Knotty' staff and one or two admiring spectators. This study commemorates what is believed to be the first occasion that town gas was used to illuminate a display hoarding, in this case decorated for the Coronation of King Edward VII.

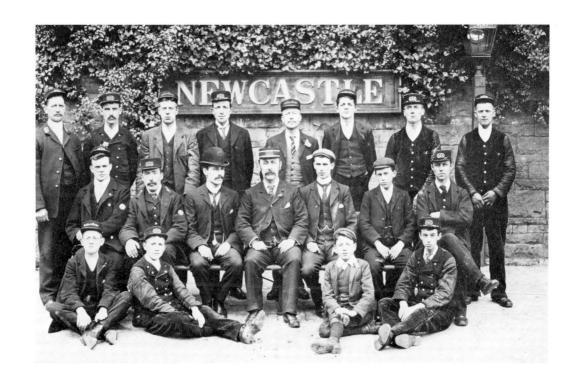

77. Station Staff, 1910 resplendent in their distinctive 'Knotty' caps.

78. Well contrived propaganda of World War II. The town acted as host to a number of Belgian refugee families throughout the 1914-1918 period. 10th November 1914 was a red-letter day for some of the Belgians, because the mayor and mayoress organised a charabanc trip for them. The run was to Swinnerton via Loggerheads and Trentham! In 1917, there was also a civic reception at the Guildhall. A Pathé Frère newsreel showing the obviously bored Belgians arriving at the outset in two very uncomfortable looking vehicles. The film was titled 'Our guests the Brave little Belgians' and screened in cinemas throughout the country.

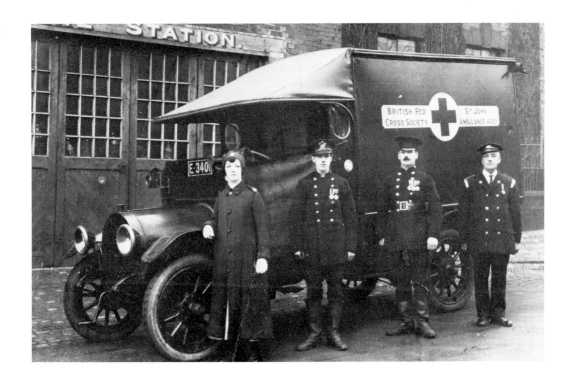

79. King Street Fire Station about 1919. An interesting print in that it records the now demolished town fire station whilst at the same time depicts the first petrol driven ambulance supplied to the local St. John Ambulance Association and Red Cross Society.

80. 'Mayor Choosing' from the Market Cross 1929. Not selected for this somewhat prosaic ceremony but the rather more interesting 'Potteries' buses in the background. The bus on the left appears still to be uncomfortably equipped with wooden seats whereas its more recent companion is luxuriously furnished in leather.

81. Obviously the P.E.T. Company could not cover the whole area with trams, it there-
fore had an auxilliary fleet of omnibuses. This is the P.E.T.'s motor bus No. 1, a splendid
Daimler with solid tyres.

82. Private bus companies were legion between the wars. Almost one hundred were operating routes in the area and competition between them was keen. Rowley's Bignall End concern ran this 'mini' bus in 1923.

83. Many of the bus companies had another regular but sadder service to operate. Unsatis-factory working conditions and general malnutrition among the poorer working class gave rise to many serious forms of respiratory disease. Tuberculosis was one very common infection which permeated society. Many local men, women and children were obliged to receive treatment and convalesce often for years at sanatoria. This inmate's snapshot shows local factory girl patients at the Loggerheads sanatorium undergoing 'fresh air therapy' in 1929.

No. 21. The Post-Office, Newcastle, Staffs.

84. Early post offices appear to have operated from inns. The earliest of these dates from 1734 and was run from the Swan Inn. High Street and Merrial Street in turn housed the general post office at various times. Until 1854 Newcastle served as the head office for the surrounding area. After this date Stoke-on-Trent, because of its railway links, assumed precedence. Newcastle had previously served all the principal pottery towns with horse drawn and foot posts. It was not until the outbreak of World War I in 1914 that the present general post office in the Ironmarket was completed. Serving the public from 1884, this card shows the principal office until it was replaced by the new one at the eastern end of the Ironmarket.

85. Now occupied by Williams & Glyn's Bank, on the corner of High Street and the Ironmarket, this was the penultimate site of the Crown office. The post office and its staff taken in 1897.

86. Rectory chambers had a considerable number of outbuildings connected with it and these remained in situ until the land they occupied was sold for Crown purposes about 1912. This was the post office site in 1910.

87. The winter of 1914 sees the post office completed. With it, the Great War brings a sad depletion of staff and the postal service has to operate under extremely difficult circumstances for the next four years.

88. All that remains of the General Post Office staff on 23rd December 1915. Most of the eligible staff had by this time either volunteered for service or been called to the colours.

89. Similar in date to the previous card, this scene in the rear yard of the post office shows that mechanisation was being introduced to speed up the delivery service. The acute shortage of labour which was now being sacrificed on the various war fronts, forced the authorities to capitalise on what remained of their workers.

90. Eastern part of the Ironmarket in the thirties. The fine boulevard and recently re-vamped Queen's Gardens create a splendid vista for shoppers entering the Ironmarket from either end. On the left of the photo can be seen the recently completed Silverdale Co-operative Society Emporium.

91. Public occasions, as with royal visits, tend to catch spectators with their guard down. Informal pictures such as these often convey the 'feel' of the occasion and indeed period far more successfully than many set pieces. When this group was taken, the 'Boer War' as it was known had been over for more than eight years and drawn to a politically unsatisfactory conclusion. Nevertheless, the town fathers in 1910 decided to honour the South African volunteers by giving them the freedom of the borough. The mayor is accompanied yet again on his right by His Imperial Highness Grand Duke Michael of Russia looking even more like a fugitive from Siberia than ever. Pomp and formality was at this time still very much the order of the day so it should come as no surprise to discover a top-hatted and morning coated reporter assiduously taking notes in the foreground.

92. One of W. Parton's splendidly detailed pictorial records showing a mayor making procession in the Ironmarket about 1909. The shop front details are worthy of close scrutiny since it is only they in most instances that have changed since this procession walked the Ironmarket.

93. Yet another formidable array of civic dignitaries and chapel leaders positioned somewhat incongruously outside the Newcastle cinema. The occasion is celebrating the Ashfield Wesleyan Mission about 1911.

94. Happily not all groups were formal or serious. This unique sepia print is of the
borough's first minstrel troupe consisting totally of local 'stars'. (1897.)

95. An ageing and a very fragile General Bramwell Booth, fighter for the 'Submerged tenth' of society visits Newcastle shortly before his death. Vast crowds turned out to greet the founder of the Salvation Army. Here he is seen at a rally in Nelson Place.

96. 'Hospital Saturday' was always a popular event in town and a great deal of hard work went into setting up stalls and floats. Designed originally to raise funds for the local Union hospitals, their scope widened as a consequence of the war to include collecting money to supply medical goods and comforts for the allies. Hospital Saturday Stall outside the Guildhall in 1908.

97. Members of a World War I Hospital Saturday float team appear to be representing one or two of the Allied Nations although who, is not quite clear.

98. Religious processions through town have never been particularly common. Apart from the regular annual Manor Making Sunday procession and service, they have rarely been recorded. This uncommon photo shows the Corpus Christi procession moving through Red Lion Square about 1925. This plate also shows the old Globe Hotel and Skerrat's the jewellers to the left.

99. On stage at the 'King's theatre', High Street. A highly colourful and quaintly dressed cast consisting of regular police and 'specials' who enacted a mock trial to raise funds for charity in March 1919.

100. Another 'still' from the Pathé film with police outside 'Carrters' and 'Mellards' family shop.

101. Like many towns, Newcastle operated its own police department until the county council became the police authority in 1947. The population explosion occasioned by the Industrial Revolution caused the authorities to re-think their crime detection policies because the crime rate and drunkenness in the town was escalating at an alarming rate. Not however until 1834 was an embryo force established. Even when it was, it only consisted of a chief officer of police, one constable and two under constables. The situation remained little improved until the eighteen seventies when at long last a concerted initiative was launched to bring the force up to government grant eligibility. From the last two decades of the nineteenth century, the force became something to be reckoned with, was well organised and capable of fighting crime reasonably well. Regulars and 'specials' muster outside the old station in 1909.

102. A well rounded body of men posing outside the 'Beeches' with the Mayor William Mellard and their chief constable William Forster on his right who was it seems not averse to writing verse when not too encumbered with police affairs.

103. Fire prevention remained the responsibility of the police until 1888 when a borough volunteer brigade came into being. It set up its headquarters in the old militia building in Barracks Road and once formed, became an autonomous service completely divorced from the police. Resplendent in their beautifully polished helmets, the borough fire team of 1901 headed by Captain Bailey, the youngest fire chief ever to be appointed in the country.

WAR HOSPITAL
STOKE-ON-TRENT.

104. The unparalleled carnage and maiming wrought during the Great War ensured that every available hospital on the home front had its wards turned over to our wounded soldiers, sailors and aviators. Parts of many civilian hospitals were completely converted to war purposes and the Newcastle Union Hospital was no exception. It was quite a common sight to see the men convalescing in their bright blue non-combatant service uniforms when on an outing to town. One of the military blocks about 1917.

105. Uniforms in war time. Quite a mixed party of wounded. One or two obviously from the North Staffordshire Regiment, but also it seems a contingent from across the Border.

NEWCASTLE STAFFS UNION HOSPITAL

106. This former military hospital, now the City General, still retains at its core the buildings which were formerly the Stoke & Wolstanton Union Workhouse and even today incorporates many structures dating from the days when Stoke parish workhouse was built in 1833. Dated 1905 here is the hospital as it appeared at the turn of the century.

107. Uniforms in peace time. O.T.C. cadets attend the funeral service of King Edward VII at St. Giles Church, 20th May 1910.

108. Uniforms on a happier occasion. Empire Day about 1927. Boys from the Newcastle High Office Training Corps marching along Marsh Parade back to school, after having taken part in the days celebrations.

Boy's High School.   Newcastle (Staffs).

109. Higher education was reorganised by the Endowed Schools Commissioners to concentrate on the provision of three basic educational establishments, a new high school, a reorganised middle school and a new girls school. Built in 1876 and unashamedly modelled on Rugby School, the Newcastle High quickly acquired an enviable academic reputation and a high proportion of its pupils regularly gained entrance to the universities. The Middle School's aim was to educate the sons of tradesmen and craftworkers whilst the Orme Girls School was designed to fulfil the growing need in late Victorian times to educate young women. The High School taken from Marsh Parade.

Memorial Chapel, Newcastle High School.

110. Classed as a 'first grade school' Newcastle High took in boarders. Initially, boys parents had to find twenty-five pounds per annum for tuition fees whilst boarders were charged an extra fifty pounds. F.E. Kitchener, the first headmaster to be appointed, had been an assistant master at Rugby and one of the school commissioners, Frederick Temple, Bishop of Exeter was at one time principal of that august public school. School chapel and assembly hall in the thirties.

111. Another 'first grade school' but this time designed specifically to educate the daughters of the 'better off'. So popular had the school become that the buildings originally planned to take one hundred girls had to be enlarged in 1886. Its first headmistress, Miss Mary Martin, had herself taught at no lesser legendary establishment than the Cheltenham Ladies College.

112. Situated in Higherland, the old Middle School or Orme Boys in 1925. Among its many pupils who were to distinguish themselves in later life was Arnold Bennett, doyen of the London literary scene in Victorian and Edwardian England.

113. G.T. Bagguley's shop photographed probably on the occasion of the visit of the Prince of Wales in 1925. This was the original frontage before the shop windows were 'modernised' in the thirties. Mr. Bagguley was a well known publisher of local views.

114. Liverpool Road in the late 1870's. Photographed by A.W. Harrison probably from outside his studio on the opposite side of the road. The whole row of houses built for the working class and now demolished were erected over a fifty year period after the old town through route from Stubbs Gate - Goose Street - Lower Street - Holborn - Lower and Upper Green had been replaced by the London Road - High Street - Liverpool Road route which came into being in 1828.

115. Luxuriously fitted out with the very latest camera gadgetery, and an artistically designed studio complete with all manner of photographic sets, this was where the Harrison family operated their photographic business. When not engaged in routine photography, A.W. Harrison produced X-ray photographs for the local hospital as and when required and appears to have been a pioneer in this field.

116. An uncommon snap of an even more uncommon advertising 'stunt' in the Liverpool Road in 1929. Hugon's 'Atora' suet van being pulled by bullocks making deliveries to its retail outlets.

J. MYOTT & SON, GENERAL DRAPERS, SILK MERCERS, ETC.

:: :: Millinery, Costumes, Dresses, :: ::
Household Drapery, Carpets and Linoleums.

46, 47 and 48, Ironmarket, and The Arcade, Cheapside,

Telephone 161.
Telegrams: "MYOTTS, Newcastle-under-Lyme. **NEWCASTLE=UNDER=LYME.**

117. J. Myott's shop on the corner of Ironmarket and Cheapside in 1912. For many years this establishment was well known in the area for its high quality merchandising and service. The shop never changed its image, maintaining throughout its existence an old fashioned approach toward retailing which eventually caused its downfall.

118. The textile mills, so long a vital part of the town's economy, have all but vanished except for the Enderly Mill. Those left are now virtually unrecognisable having in the main been re-built or changed out of all recognition to suit the needs of twentieth century trade. Formerly the Brampton Silk Mill in Hempstalls Lane, depicted here derelict after a spell as a boot factory and then a fustian mill after silk throwing had ceased. The premises have now been resurrected into a photographic wholesale warehouse. It can still just be recognised as a former silk mill.

119. There were not many people living in the town between the wars who did not know Mr. Chadwick, the antique dealer, and his shop. One of the houses in this long disappeared row of nineteenth century properties removed to make way for the new civic offices, contained his shop in Merrial Street. The debris in the foreground marks the spot where a once busy colony of hatters and feltmakers plied their trade.

120. Church Street and Red Lion Square corner opposite St. Giles' Church entrance about 1896. The technological revolution has arrived! or so claims the window display created by the International Correspondence Schools of London. 'Improve your memory and earn more money if you enrol in our correspondence course.' Such institutions abounded at this time given impetus no doubt by the 1870 Education Act which had provided a basic education for the masses a couple of decades or so previously. At least they could now read what the 'ads' had to say.

121. Lad Lane with the old post office on the extreme left.

122. Goodall and Hargreaves, High Street Auction Rooms and furniture emporium 1895. Before its total demise this building was converted into the 'Regal and Pavilion' cinemas later to be known as the Rex and Rio. See plate seven.

123. Early morning in Red Lion Square probably in readiness for Queen Victoria's diamond jubilee celebrations. On the right can be seen the town's old weights & measures office which was first sited to the south of the Guildhall in 1835 but removed here in 1876. It was destroyed in 1926.

124. Finally, the town poised for greater things! This mayor choosing group, one of the last to be taken before the borough extended its boundaries in 1932, shows many of the members of the council who were destined to steer the borough through the troubled waters of re-organisation and expansion. A daunting task, since the population more than doubled from 23,000 in 1930 to 54,000 a couple of years later.